Kings

Also by Christopher Logue

WAR MUSIC

KINGS

An Account of
Books 1 and 2
of Homer's *Iliad*

Christopher Logue

Farrar · Straus · Giroux

New York

Library of Congress Cataloging-in-Publication Data
Logue, Christopher.
Kings : an account of books one and two of Homer's Iliad /
Christopher Logue. — 1st American ed.
1. Homer—Adaptations.   2. Achilles (Greek mythology)—Poetry.
3. Trojan War—Poetry.   I. Title.
PR6023.038K5   1991   821'.914—dc20   91-12936 CIP

Excerpts from Kings have been published in The Paris Review, The Fred, Scripsi,
Bête Noire, and The Poetry Book Society Anthology 1989–1990.

All performing rights in this work are
fully protected and permission to perform
in whole or in part must be obtained in
advance in writing from Christopher Logue's agent,
Susan Bergholz, 340 West 72nd Street,
New York, NY 10023

To Rosemary Hill

Contents

Introduction

In this book I have gone about things in the same way as I did with *War Music*, whose introduction explains the recipe in detail. That is to say, I have concocted a storyline based, in this case, on the main incidents of the *Iliad's* first two books, added a scene or two of my own, and then, knowing no Greek but having got from translations made in the accepted sense of the word the gist of what this or that character said, attempted to make their voices come alive, and to keep the action on the move.

Not, therefore, a proper translation, but what I hope will turn out to be a poem in English dependent on the *Iliad*, whose composition is reckoned to have preceded the beginnings of our own written language by fifteen centuries.

For critical, and financial, support while writing *Kings* I am much indebted: for the first, to Liane Aukin, who clarified the text and who will—all things being equal—direct the performance version; to Craig Raine, who has been what I have never yet had, a critical editor, and one who made many improvements; and to Lindsay Anderson and Michael Hastings; for the second, to Mr. Raymond Danowski, Bernard Pomerance, and Lord Weidenfeld; to the Arts Council of Great Britain, the Drama (Radio) Department of the BBC, and the Society of Authors.

May I also thank those who wrote, or spoke, to others on my behalf: firstly, Shusha Guppy; also, Charles Rowan Beye, Robert Fogarty, Jasper Griffin, John Gross, Philip Howard, Christian Hesketh, Andrew Motion, Kathleen Tynan, and my friend Bernard Stone.

And last, though he is not speaking to me at the moment (and is therefore responsible for all that is wrong with what follows), Professor Donald Carne-Ross of Boston University.

Kings

Prologue

Helen left Greece for Ilium in the company of Paris, the son of Priam, king of Troy.

To repossess her, the Greeks, led by Agamemnon, gathered 1,000 ships, sailed to Troy, and, while fighting to overcome Hector's defence of that city, maintained themselves by raiding Ilium's lesser towns.

However, after one such raid, Agamemnon's overbearingness caused Achilles, his best warrior, to withdraw from the fight: and this was bad. But worse, Achilles ran to the beach and asked his goddess mother, Thetis of the Sea, to make God side with Troy against the Greeks, and so to change the course of history.

1

Picture the east Aegean sea by night,
And in an open bay before that sea
Upwards of 30,000 men
Asleep like spoons among their fatal ships.
  Now look along the moonlit beach, and note
A naked man, face wet with tears,
Run with what seems to break the speed of light
Across the dry, then damp, then sand invisible
Beneath inch-high waves that slide
Over each other's luminescent panes;
Then kneel among those panes, beggar his arms, and pray:

  "Out of humiliation, Source, I cry,
Source, hear my voice, and with your presence
Bless my supplication."

  The sea as quiet as light.
His voice flows on:

  "God is your debtor, Source.
He put you in my father's bed. And to redeem
Such ignominious miscegenation
Swore that if I, the only child that you would bear,
Chose to die young, by violence, alone,
In some forgotten corner of the world,
My honour should, where honour means
The recognition of superiority,
Be first, be best, the best of bests,
The most astonishing that fame shall light,
Here, and in perpetuity.

And so I chose. Nor have I changed. But now—
By which I mean today, this instant, *now*—
The one plain King, our God, the Shepherd of the Clouds,
Sees me humiliated through the camp
Clearly as if he sent a hand to shoo
The army into one, and then, before its eyes,
Painted my body with fresh Trojan excrement."

Sometimes
Before the gods appear
Something is marked:
    A noise. A note, perhaps. Perhaps
A change of temperature. Or else, as now,
The scent of oceanic lavender,
That even as it drew his mind
Drew from the seal-coloured sea onto the beach
A mist that moved like weed, then stood, then turned
Into his mother, Thetis', mother lovelost face,
Her fingers, next, that lift his chin, that push
His long, redcurrant-coloured hair
Back from his face, her voice, her words:

"Why tears, Achilles?
Rest in my arms and answer from your heart."

    And the sea, so still
It looks like metal plate.

"Three weeks ago," he said, "while raiding southern Ilium
I killed the men and stripped a town called Tollo
Whose yield comprised a wing of Hittite chariots
And 30 fertile women.
    As is required
The latter reached the beach-head unassigned,

8

Were sorted by the herald's staff, and then
Soon after sunrise on the following day
Led to the common sand for distribution.
  At which point, mother mine"—his tears have gone—
"Enter the king. No-no. Our king of kings, majestic Agamemnon,
His nose extruded from his lionshead cowl,
Its silvered claws clasped so"—arms over chest—
"And sloping up his shoulder, thus, the mace,
The solar mace, that stands for—so I thought—
What Greeks require of Greeks:
  To worship God; to cherish honour;
To fight courageously, keeping your own,
And so, the status of your fellow lords
High, mother, high—as he knows well—as he knew well—
As he came walking through those culled
By acclamation when the best
Assemble for the herald Stentor's 'Who is owed?'
Into the pen of captured shes,
Here sniffing, pinching here, lifting a lip, a lid,
Asking his brother: 'One, Menelaos, or . . . or two?'
  Then, having scanned their anxious faces with his own,
The guardian of our people outs the mace
As if it was a mop, and with its gold
Egg-ended butt, selects—before the owed—
A gently broken adolescent she
Who came—it seemed—from plain but prosperous ground."

  "First king, first fruit," his mother said.
  "Will you hear more, or not?" he said.
  "Dear child . . ."
  "Then do not interrupt."

  The stars look down.
Troy is a glow behind the dunes.
  The camp is dark.

9

"Her name was Cryzia," Achilles said.
"Less than a week
After she went through Agamemnon's gate,
Her father, Cryzez of Cape Tollomon,
The archpriest of Apollo's coastal sanctuary,
Came to the beach-head, up, between the ships,
Holding before him, outright, with both hands,
An ivory rod adorned with streams of wool,
Twice consecrated to that Lord of Light.
   Pausing an instant by Odysseus' ship—
Our centrepoint—
He reached the middle of the common sand, and,
With the red fillets blowing round his shaven head,
Waited until its banks were packed,
Then offered all, but principally
King Agamemnon and his queenless brother,
Two shipholds of amphorae filled with Lycian wine,
A fleet of Turkey mules,
2,000 sheepskins, cured, cut, and sewn,
To have his daughter back: plus these gloved words:

   'Paramount Agamemnon, King of Kings,
Lord of both Mainland and of Island Greece,
May Zeus Almighty grant that you,
And those who follow you,
Demolish Troy, then sail safe home.
   Only take these commodities for my child,
So tendering your mercy to God's son,
Apollo, Lord of Light and Mice.'

   'Yes!'
   'Yes!'
   'Yes!'
   'Yes!'

"The Fighters cried,
And Yes to them—but to themselves—the lords.

"You would have thought the matter done.
A bargain; with himself—
Well over 40 if a day—
Having had, and then released, a dozen such
For general use.
    But no.
Before the fourth Yes died our guardian lord began:

    'As my pronouncement will affect you all,
Restrain your Yessings,' and when we did so,
    'If,' he continues, 'if, priest, if
When I complete the things I am about to say,
I catch you loitering around my Fleet
Ever again, I shall, with you in one,
And in my other hand your mumbo rod,
Thrash you until your eyeballs shoot.
    As for your child:
Bearing by night my body in my bed,
Bearing by day my children on her knee,
Soft in the depths of my ancestral house,
If ever she sees Ilium again
She will have empty gums.
    Be safe—be gone. For good.'

"Fearful as the toad in a python's mouth,
The priest, as if the world was empty, walked away
Beside the cold, great, grey-mouthed, incomprehending sea,
Then hung his head
And prayed wet-cassocked in the foam:

    '*Mousegod*,

Whose reach makes distance myth,
In Whose abundant warmth
The vocal headlands of Cape Tollomon bask,
As all my life I dressed Your leafy shrine
And have, with daily holocausts,
Honoured Your timeless might,
Vouchsafe me this:
For every hair upon my daughter's head
Let ten Greeks die.' "

Barely a pace
Above the Mediterranean's dim edge
Mother and child.
    And as she asks: "Then what?"
Their early pietà dissolves to black,
And though their voices stay,
Knowing what he will say
We do not strain to catch his words,
    And soon
Only motionless rivers and moonlit dunes
Lie in-between ourselves
And holy Troy.

                    •

Long after midnight when you park, and stand
Just for a moment in the chromium wash,
Sometimes it seems that, some way off,
Between the river and the tower belt, say,
The roofs show black on pomegranate red,
As if, below that line, they stood in fire.

Lights similar to these were seen
By those who looked from Troy towards the Fleet
After Apollo answered Cryzez' prayer.

Taking a corner of the sky
Between his finger and his thumb,
Out of its blue, as boys do towels, he cracked,
Then zephyr ferried in among the hulls
A generation of infected mice.

Such fleas . . .
Such lumps . . .
Watch Greece begin to die:

Busy in his delirium, see Tek
(A carpenter from Mykonos) as he comes forward, hit—
It seems—by a stray stone, yet still comes on,
Though coming now as if he walked a plank,
Then falling off it into nothingness.
    See 20—dead in file,
Their budded tongues crystallized with green fur,
As daily to the fire-pits more cart more,
As half, it seemed, incinerated half,
And sucking on their masks
The cremators polluted Heaven.

"Home . . ."
"Home . . ."

Nine days of this,
And on the tenth, Ajax,
Grim underneath his tan as Rommel after 'Alamein,
Summoned the army to the common sand,
Raised his five-acre voice, and said:

"Fighters!
Hear what my head is saying to my heart:

"The Trojans, or the mice, will finish us,

13

Unless Heaven helps.
We are not short of those who see beyond the facts.
Some dreams, some thoughts, they say, are sent by God.
Let them advise.
High smoke can make amends."

He sits.
Our quietude assents.
Ajax is loved. I mean it. He is *loved*.
Not just for physical magnificence
(The eyelets on his mesh like runway lights)
But this: no Greek—including Thetis' son—
Contains a heart so brave, so resolute, so true,
As this gigantic lord from Salamis.

The silence thickens.
Eyes slide, then slide away, then slide again
Onto the army's eldest augur, Calchas, who,
With the panoramic tone of those that see
Is, was, and will
As easily as other men the moon,
Half rose, and having said:

"The Lord of Light finds Greece abominable,"
Half sat, sat, looked about, shirked Agamemnon's eye,
Caught ten as lordly, re-arose, and said:

"Kings lose their heads, but not their memories.
Who will protect me if I say
What Agamemnon does not want said?"

"Me,"

Said Achilles,
As he stood.

"Begin when I have sworn."

Then lifts his palms and says:

"This before God:
From Ethiopia to Thrace,
From Babylon to the Hesperides,
As high—as low—as Idan peaks, or the Aegean's floor,
While I am still alive and killing, no one shall touch
You, sir, or anybody here who can say why
The Lord of Light finds Greece abominable—
And, sir, no one includes our self-appointed first,
Best king, Lord Agamemnon of Mycenae."

Then sat beside his friend, his next, his heart,
Patroclus, lord Menotion's son,
While Calchas said:

"The sacred vermin came because
King Agamemnon menaced Lord Apollo's priest.
Because King Agamemnon will not give that priest,
Though offered more than due,
His soft-topped-eyed and squashed-mouth daughter back.
    Nor will they boil away
Until Lord Agamemnon, dueless now,
Resigns that daughter to her father's stock,
With these winged words:
    Resume your child in Heaven's name,
And may the high smoke from the sacrifice
Of these 200 perfect sheep
Propitiate the Lord of Mice and Light."

Low ceiling. Sticky air.
Many draw breath,
As Agamemnon, red with rage, yells:

15

"Blindmouth!
Good words would rot your tongue."
    Then reads the warning in his brother's face,
And says (half to himself):
    "Well, well, well, well . . .
You know your way around belief."
    Then looking out:
    "Greece knows I want this girl
More than I want the father-given, free-born she
Who rules Mycenae in my place—Greek Clytemnestra.
Although, unlike that queen, the girl has not
Parted a boy to bear my honoured name,
Yet as she stitches, stands, and speaks as well,
Raised to the rank of wife, so might she suckle."

    The army breathes again.

    "However,
As being first means being privileged,
So privilege incurs responsibility.
And my responsibility is plain:
To keep the army whole. To see it hale.
To lead it through the Skean Gate."

    Again.

    "Therefore,
With the addition of a Cretan bull,
To our religious entertainer's charge,
The girl shall be returned to Tollomon."

    Applause.

    The lord of Crete, Idomeneo, starts to slip away.

16

"But . . ."

Then stops.

". . . as the loss of an allotted she
Diminishes my honour and my state,
Before the army leaves the common sand
Its lords will find, among their own,
Another such for me."

Low ceiling. Sticky air.
Our stillness like the stillness
In Atlantis as the big wave came,
The brim-full basins of abandoned docks,
Or Christmas morning by the sea.

Until Achilles said:

"Dear Sir,
Where shall we get this she?
There is no pool.
We land. We fight. We kill. We load. And then—
After your firstlings—we allot.
That is the end of it.
We do not ask things back. And even you
Would not permit your helmet to go round.
     Leave her to Heaven.
And when—and if—God lets me leap Troy's Wall
Greece will restock your dormitory."

"Boy Achilleus," Agamemnon said,
"You will need better words
And more than much more charm
Before your theorizing lightens me.

Myself unshe'd, and yours still smiling in the furs?
Ditchmud."

And widening his stare:
"Consult. Produce a string. Cryzia was fit
To be covered by a god. So pick your tenderest. Or—
Now listen carefully—
I shall be at your gate, lord Ajax, or
Entering yours, intrepid Diomed, or
Once within yours, truth's pet, Achilles-san—
Kah!—What does it matter whose prize she I take?
But take I shall, and if needs be, by force.

"Well . . .
We shall see.

"And now
Let us select and stow a ship,
Captained by you, lord Thoal, or by you,
Our silencer, Idomeneo,
At all events some diplomatic lord
To take my pretty Cryzia home,
That holy smoke and thermal prayers
May exorcize the insects we refresh."

Then turned, and would have gone except
Achilles strode across the sand towards him,
One arm up, jabbing his fist into the sky, as:
"Mouth! King mouth!" he called,
And set his tungsten look
Straight down the line of Agamemnon's own.
Then stopped.
Then from the middle of the sand, said:

"Heroes, behold your king—

18

Slow as an arrow fired feathers first
To puff another's worth,
But watchful as a cockroach of his own.
    Behold his cause—
Me first, me second,
And if by chance there is a little left—me third.
    Behold his deeds—
Fair ransom scanted, and its donor spurned.
The upshot—plague.
    O Agamemnon, O King Great I Am,
The Greeks who follow you; who speak for you;
Who stand among the blades for you;
Prostitute loyalty.
    To me, the Ilians are innocent.
They have not fleeced my father's countryside.
Cloud-shadowing mountains and abyssal seas
Separate them from Pythia. And half the time
You Mycenean / Trojans seem to me
Like two bald men fighting over a comb.
    If steal is right, my king,
It was a Spartan, not a Pythic wife
Cock Paris lifted from your brother's bed;
Your hospitality that platinum maggot slimed;
Your name, not mine, he sacked; and yours, not mine,
The battles *I* have sited, fought, and won.
    'Well . . . We shall see.' Indeed.
Zero to zero. Dead cells. Shredded. Gone.

    "Since I arrived, my lord,
I have sent 20 lesser Ilian towns
Backwards into the smoke.
But—when, as required, we distribute—
To you the delicates, to me, the dottle of their loss—
Except for her, Briseis, my ribbon she,
Whose fearless husband, plus some 50

19

Handsome-bodied warriors I killed and burned
At Thebé-under-Ida as it burned
And so was named her owner by you all
In recognition of my strength, my courage, my superiority.

"Well then, my lord,
You change the terms, I change the tense.
    Let is be was. Was the day on which
Backlit by long-necked flames
You lead your Greeks, necklaced with spoil,
Capering along the road that tops Troy's Wall:
Because you cannot take the city without me.
Me. Pe'leus' son.
Because tomorrow, I sail home."

    Reverse the shot. Go close.
Hear Agamemnon, Lord of lords, Autarch of Argos,
Whose eminent domain includes all southern Greece:

    "Many will say,
Good riddance to bad rubbish.
I shall not.
    I am your king.
God called. God raised. God recognized.
    Nestor, Odysseus, Ajax,
Cretan Idomeneo, Diomed,
Thoal of Calydon, Mica of Thessaly,
Stand at my name.
    Look at them, boy. They are not muck.
They have been here nine years.
When you were what?—a bubble on a dam.
Likewise the thousands in whose sight we stand.
They honour me. And I am popular.
    God made you fast. Some say the fastest. And some say
More beautiful than any other man.

Indubitably he made you strong, and brave.
　So tell me this: who made you sour?
For you are sour, boy Achilleus, sour.
　The time has come for you to see
More of your family.
And I am confident that he will find—
And we shall hear that he has found—
Honour as lasting in his cuckoo woods
As that he won at Troy."
　Then to them all:
　"Here is the news.
Before world-class Achilles leaves for home,
As God has taken Cryzia from myself
I shall take his best she, Briseis, from him.
　More.
Her confiscation shows, once and for all,
My absolute superiority,
Not just to you, retiring boy, but anyone
Stupid enough to challenge me
In word or deed."

　Achilles' face
Is like a chalkpit fringed with roaring wheat.
His brain says: "Kill him. Let the Greeks sail home."
His thigh steels flex.

　And then,
Like a match-flame struck in full sunlight,
We lose him in the prussic glare
Goddess Athena, called the Woman Prince—who burst
Howling and huge out of Zeus' head—sheds
From her hard, wide-apart eyes, as she enters
And stops time.

　But those still dying see:

Achilles leap the 15 yards between
Himself and Agamemnon;
Achilles land, and straighten up, in one;
Achilles' fingertips—such elegance!—
Push push-push push, push Agamemnon's chest;
The king back off; Achilles grab
And twist the mace out of his royal hand,
And lift it . . . Oh . . . flash! flash!
The heralds running up . . .

   But we stay calm,
For we have seen Athena's radiant hand
Collar Achilles' plait, and then,
As a child its favourite doll,
Draw his head slowly back towards her lips
And say:

   "You know my voice?
   You know its power?

   "Be still.

   "Hera has sent me. As God's wife, she said:
'Stop him. I like them both.'
   I share her view. In any case
We have arranged another death for Agamemnon.
If you can stick to speech, harass him now.
But try to kill him, and I kill you.

   She goes,
And time restarts.

   The mace.
King Agamemnon outs his hand.

Palm up.
  Achilles says:

  "I hate your voice, claw king. I hate its tune.
Lord of All Voices is God's fairest name.
Your voice defiles that name. Cuntstruck Agamemnon!—
The king who would use force against his lord.
  O cheesey Lung,
I know as much, in likelihood much more,
About the use of force as any here,
Master or muster, first or flock, hero or host,
And in my backwood way have half a mind
To knock you multinational flat with this"—
His hand—"then bar your throat with this"—his foot—
"Kingman who never yet led star or store
Into the blades, or kept them there,
Or raised his blade alone—for no one doubts
That Hector, the councillor of Priam's 50 sons,
Would, if you raised it, see your arm.
  Kih! I forgot. Our king is philosophical;
He fears his youth has gone; he will not fight, today.
Tomorrow, then? Tomorrow we will see.
Indeed, boy Achilleus—as my dear father says—
Boy Achilleus, you are wrong to criticize.
Atreus is king. What need has he to keep
A helicopter whumphing in the dunes,
Being popular, with heroes at his heel?

  "My lords.
I was too young to take the oath you swore
When Helen's father said:
  'This womb is now a wife,'
And handed her to you, brave Menelaos.
But each one vowed:

23

If she, our loveliest,
Is stolen, or she strays,
As we are all her husbands,
Each one of us, heedless of cost,
Will be in honour bound to win her back.

"So here you are.

"Shame that your king is not so bound to you
As he is bound to what he sniffs, and bound to mute
The voice that hints, just hints, he might be, um . . .
Not wrong, of course, ah . . . how shall we put it?—
A hair's-breadth less than absolutely right.

"Here is the truth:
King Agamemnon is not honour bound.
Honour to Agamemnon is a thing
That he can pick, pick up, put back, pick up again,
A somesuch you might find beneath your bed.
    Do not tell Agamemnon honour is
No mortal thing, but ever in creation,
Vital, free, like speed, like light,
Like silence, like the gods!
The movement of the stars! Beyond the stars!
Dividing man from beast, hero from host,
That proves best, best, that only death can reach,
Yet cannot die because it will be said, be sung,
Now, and in time to be, for evermore."

"Amen."
"He is so beautiful."
"Without him we are lost."
Thoal, then Menelaos, then Odysseus said
(But only to themselves) as he swept on:

24

"I do not fear you, King. Your voice is false,"
Then lifts his arm and makes a T—
    "You tax where you should tender, feed where fend"—
Out of its upright, with the mace as bar.
    "This mace objectifies custom and truth.
Hephaestus, the Lame Lord of Fire,
Made it to glorify our Father, God,
When cosmos conquered chaos at his touch.
Bronze trimmed its haft. Its roots are coal.
Mortals who tote it are required to bring
Fair judgement out of Heaven to earth.
    By it, hear this:
Call at our gate, King; my Patroclus will
Surrender Briseis. Touch else of ours—
Then I will snap your back across my knee.
    But from this moment on,
Seeing your leadership has left me leaderless,
I shall not fight for you, or by your side,
Or for, or by, these nothing lords that let you live.
    Those who believe that I am in the right,
Speak now: or never speak to me again."

No sound.

Lord Thoal thinks: "Boy, boy,
You have not heard a word of what he said;
And in a moment you will say
Our silence has betrayed you."

No sound.

A whinny. Wings. The wheezing of the sea.
And so he craned his wrist,
Watched the mace fall into the sand,
And kept his face towards it.

25

No sound.

And still no sound.

Then
Drinking his tears,
Achilles called into the sky:

"Which will you see, great clouds?
World-famous Troy fall to his voice,
Or Greece to pieces in his hands?"
    And wiping them away:
    "You lords will be his widows. Tiger bait.
Down plain, or in the dunes there, kie!
Kie! Troy has come. Aeneas and Prince Paris come,
Moved on your fleet by music, trumpets come,
In one wide cry of rage, Sarpedon come.
The sea will ring with it. The sea will clap its hands.
And Hector, yes, his shout alone will burst you wide.
Then neither ditch, ramp, main camp track,
Nor double row of ships that drape the bay,
Headland to headland, will protect your knees
As you run down the beach.
    Please do not say
'When sorrow comes Achilles will relent.'
Witness me glad. Yes. Glad. Extra glad when
Longing for me makes every one of you
Reach in his own broad chest,
Take out, and suck, his heart,
Then spit its extract in his neighbour's face,
Ashamed, that you, the Panachean lords,
Dishonoured and betrayed lord Achilleus,
The best of the Acheans."

The world is shut.

Talthibios, chief herald of the Greeks,
Nods to a lesser indeterminate
Who lifts and takes the mace to Agamemnon,
And bow-backs-out before that king concludes:

"Thank you, Greece.
As is so often true,
Silence has won the argument.
Achilles speaks as if I found you on a vase.
So leave his stone-age values to the sky."

A few loose claps,
And those around the muster's voice,
Thersites of Euboea, say
(Not all that loudly):
    "I told you so."
    "Shame . . ."
    "Home . . ."

Silence again.

And as Achilles strode away, Patroclus stood
And followed close without a word.

•

Low on the hillsides to the east of Troy,
Women, waist-deep in dusk, shoulder their baskets
And, ascending, see the Wall's black edge
Level the slopes it covers and demand
Fires in the linen city at its foot;
And over all, riding a lake of tiles,
The Temple on the sunset-lit acropolis
Whose columns stripe the gilded arrowhead
The rivers Sy'mois and Scamander make

As they meet, whose point flows out, flows on, until,
Imagined more than seen,
King Agamemnon's army stands,
As in the sepias of Gallipoli,
Thigh-deep, chest-deep,
Heaping the level ocean's ember blue
Over their curls, over their shoulders, as they pray:
    "Dear Lord of Light, reclaim Your mice,"
And stately through their faces, oars aloft,
Blonde Cryzia wreathed beneath its scorpion tail,
By her the ox: *"Dear Lord of Light,"*
The tribute ship is handed south.

•

Moist wind. Black wind. Rainbearing wind.
The tents like lanterns; green beneath dark hulls.
    Walking between them, lower lip upthrust,
The corners of his mouth pulled down, Nestor,
The lord of Sandy Pylos, cloaked and calm,
Past 80 if a day:
    "To see,"
Accompanied by his son, Antilochos,
    "Achilles."

Nod.
Look.
The gate.
The compound.
Then:

"Wait for me here."

No stars.

Redcurrant hair seats white.

Dark wine in gold.

A sip.

Then, setting it down:

"Shame on you both.
And more on you than him.
   I did not come this far to hear
That Troy is innocent.
   Troy is not innocent.
   Troy lies.
   Troy steals.
   Troy harbours thieves.

"You are the same age as my son.
He worships you. Ask him,
That boy will follow you through arrowfire like rain.
Had you been Pylian I would have kinged
Not only you, and him who fathered you,
But who sired him. So learn:
   Far better men than you have seen the sky,
And I have fought beside, and saved, their like;
And I have fought against, and killed, their like;
And when the fight was done I told them how
Victors should act; and they obeyed me.
   You are a child in parliament.
Someone talks common-nonsense and—tarrah!—
You give his words a future. Let them die.
You swear; and you are sworn. The world must change.
Speak to the gods if you want change.
   Great people promise more than they can do.
And you expect too much from promising.

29

Think of our offerings to each other.
Our past. Our partings. Our close dead.
Your 'Troy is innocent' betrays them.
'Tell him that . . .' Yes I will.
So feed your patience.
    But when I do
I shall not put my finger in his face,
But on the gift I bring.
    Be still!
Do not tell me he has enough.
I know he has enough.
But that is how he is. Requiring.
Furthermore—it is his due.
    The mace was left to him.
He lords more men, more land, more sea,
Than any other Greek.
You are part dust, part deity.
But he is king. And so, for Greece, comes first.
    Honour his rank, honour your name.
But as Thersites' eczema words
Put off our taking Troy by putting 'Home!' 'Home!' 'Home!'
Into the army's mind, your 'Home' eggs his,
And all the other gash that tumbles out
Of his sisal-ball head.
    Thersites of Euboea, blustering rat;
Pe'leus' son, Achilles;
To link them in a sentence is to lie."

Their shadows on the textile.

"Think of the day when I and Ajax drove
Out of the trees towards Pe'leus' house
And waited in its gateway while he poured
Bright wine along the thigh-cuts off a steer
Just sacrificed to Zeus—guardian

30

Of kings, of guests—when you,
Noticing us and springing up in one,
Ran to the gateway, took our hands, and led us in.
Kind boy. Good boy . . . And then,
When all had had enough to eat and drink,
Big Ajax asked if you and your dear heart,
Patroclus, could join the Greeks at Troy,
And he said yes. Then eyed you up and down,
And told you: One: to be the best.
To stand among the blades where honour grows,
Where fame is won, untouched by fear.
Counting on Hera and Athene for your strength—
If they so will. And Two: to mind your tongue.'

They sip.

Gold holly in the hearth.

"Achilles, you are like my own.
Spirit, and strength, and beauty have combined
Such awesome power in you,
A vacant Heaven would offer you its throne.
    If I, your grounded honourer,
Persuade the king to leave things as they are,
Briseis still your she, and no more said,
Will you be as you were—our edge?
    Look in my eyes, and answer."

Host.

And guest.

Patroclus to Achilles' left. His face kept down.

Firelight against a painted chest.

31

10,000 miles away
A giant child rests her chin on the horizon
And blows a city down.

Then a new voice:

"Father."
"I ordered you to wait."
"The King has sent Talthibios for Briseis."

Silence.

The lamps lap oil.

"Fetch her, Patroclus," Achilles said.
And then:
"Time-honored lord of Pylos,
Your voice is honey and your words are winged.
I hope we meet again."

Then to his porch.

Talthibios and E'thyl on their hams.
Then, taking Talthibios' elbow in his hand:

"Medium of truth, do not embarrass me.
I know that you have no share in the blame."

And when they stood, but back, well back,
As normals do when facing him:

"Patroclus will bring her.
Tell those who ask I meant my words.
    I hate their king. He is a needle in my bread.

He is water! I am air! I honour you. Go.
Go."

    And when he was alone, he soiled himself,
His body and his face, with ash.
Then, naked, wet with tears,
Ran with what seemed to break the speed of light
To call his mother from the sea;
As we have seen.

                              •

    The beach.
The wind is up. The moonlit sea,
Like plate.

    Observe their walk. The goddess, Thetis, small
And sadly sensual; turning her lavish face
Upsideways to her frightening son,
Whose ash-streaked arm arches her shoulders, down her side,
Who says, and says, and says:

    "That is the whole of it. The Greeks have let
Their Agamemnon grab my prize she.
    So go to God.
Press him. Yourself against him. Kiss his knees.
Then beg him this:
    Till they come running on their knees to me,
Pe'leus' son, your only child,
Let the Greeks burn, let them taste pain,
Asphyxiate their hope, so as their blood soaks down into the sand,
Or as they sink like rings into the sea,
They learn."

    "I love you, child. But we are caught.

You will die soon. And sadly. And alone.
While I shall live for ever with my tears.
Keep your hate warm. God will agree," his mother said

       And walked into the waves
As he went up the beach towards his ship,
Towards the two great armies, all asleep.

                           •

       Water, white water, blue-black here, without—
Us hearing our bow wave—
Our animals hearing those closest ashore.
       Swell-water, black-water—
The wind in the cliff pines, their hairpins, their resin,
And—
As we glide through their cleft—
The sea—
Suddenly warm and sky blue, as the light
Dives and returns from the sand—
As we lower, lose way, set, stroke, and regain it—
Then pace the wide still ring
Of Cape Tollomon's answering bay—
At our peak—(now we ship)—
With lord Thoal's hand on her shoulder—
Cryzia, her eyes in her father's, and him—
With many—(his choir, his dancers)—"Sing Ave!"—
His eyes in his daughter's—"Sing Ave!"—and then,
As Thoal hands her ashore,
    "Sing Ave!"
    "Sing Ave!"
Once more in his arms.

       And when that solemn time had passed:

"Priest of Apollo's coastal sanctuary,"
Lord Thoal said,
"The Lord of Mainland and of Island Greece,
Paramount Agamemnon, my true king,
Bid me to lead your child into your arms.
   Thereafterwards,
That their high smoke, and our encircling prayers
Appease the one whose vermin Greece infects,
Joint-voiced, we sacrifice these lovely animals
To God's first son, Apollo born,
The Lord of Light and Mice."

                              •

   The altar is oval, made of red quartz,
And broad-leaved plane trees shade the turf it crowns.
   Hear them come!
"Let the Greeks bring the knife,"
   Here they come!
By the stream that freshens the bearded grass,
   "To slit the white-socked ox's throat,"
Wading the orchids that verge the turf,
   "And we will carry the bowls
Of mountain water and sainted wine,
And the axe."
   "Pae'an!"
   Hear their song!
As their pale feet darken the fragrant turf,
   "Pae'an!"

   They have come.

   See the ox at the stone.
"Lord of Light!"
   See its gilded horns.

"Lord of Light!"
See the axe.

Now the lustral water is on their hands,
And the barley sprinkled on the beast's wide head.
"Bring the axe."
"Pae'an!"
"Lord of Mice!"
"Lord of Light! Light! Light!"
As the axe swings up, and stays,
"Pae'an!"
Stays poised, still poised, and—
As it roars down:
"PLEASE GOD!"
"PLEASE GOD!"
Covers the terrible thock that parts the ox from its voice

"Pae'an!"

As the knife goes in, goes down
And the dewlap parts like glue,
And the great thing kneels,
And its breath hoses out,
And the authorized butchers grope for its heart,
And the choir sings:

"Pour the oil and balm—"

And Cryzez prays:

"O Lord of Light
Whose reach makes distance myth
In Whose abundant warmth
The headlands of Cape Tollomon bask,"
"Over the dead—"

"As all my life I dressed Your leafy shrine,"
"Fire the cedar, fire the clove—"
  "Vouchsafe me this:"
"That the reek may lie—"
  "Absolve the Greeks,"
"And the savour lift—"
  "Let the plague die,"
"To Heaven, and to yourself."
  "Amen."
  "Amen."

Were we deceived—or did
The ox consent with a shake of its head,
And the sunlight brighten, as Cryzez prayed?
Either way, the women sang:
  "Child   Child of Light   We beg,"
Then the men:
    "Heed the thirst in our song!"

  "Lord   Lord of Light   We beg,"
And the men:
    "Feel the need in our song!"

  "Lord   Lord of Mice   We pray,"
    "Let the plague die!
    Let the plague die!"

  We sang
And made the day divine.

  High smoke from oil-drenched ox tripes stood in Heaven.
Leaves of lean meat spat on the barbecues.
Silver took sea-dark wine from lip to lip.
Flutes. Anklets. Acorn bells. The shameless air.
Enough for all.

And then, when, simultaneously,
The moon lit this side and the sun lit that
Side of the blades they lifted to salute
The Evening Star,
Safe in Apollo's custody they slept,
Sailed on Aurora's breath
Over the shaggy waves;
Regained their war;
Heard that the plague had gone: were glad:
And said goodbye to one another
In sight of Troy's dark Wall.

　　　　　　　•

But Achilles was not glad.
Each moment of each minute of the day,
　Let the Greeks die,
　Let them taste pain,
Remained his prayer.
　And he for who
Fighting was breath, was bread,
Remained beside his fatal ships,
Below the bay's west head,
And hurt his honour as he nursed his wrong.

　　　　　　　•

GOD LIVES FOR EVER.

Come quickly, child! There! There!
Salute him with your eyes!

Brighter than day, his shadow; silent as light
The footprint of his time-free flight
Down the Nile's length, across the Inland Sea

To Paradise Olympus where it rides
High on the snowy lawns of Thessaly,
And an unpleasant surprise is waiting for him:

Thetis,
Wearing the beady look of motherhood,
Who starts right in
(Before his feet scarce touch the ground):

"God of All Gods, Most Holy, and Most High,"
And then reminds him of her conscientiousness;
Then (seating him) of her enforced, demeaning, coitus;
Then of his nodded promise (as she keeps his hand)
Made to her son:
"If you, my Thetis' only child,
Choose to die young, by violence, alone,
Your honour will be recognized as best,
The most astonishing that fame shall light,
Now, or in perpetuity."
Then (twining her arms behind his knees)
She ends:
"I must have Yes or No.
If Yes, repeat these words:
In honour of your son
Whose honour has been blighted by his king,
In that that king has grabbed his honour she,
I will take Hector's part until
The Greeks are soaked in blood from head to foot—
Then fatalize this promise with your nod.
If No, I am a lost bitch barking at a cloud."

A crease has formed between God's eyes.
His silence hurts.
Over his suppliant's tar-dark hair

He sees the ascension of the Evening Star
Beckon infinity. And says:

"Goddess,
I am in trouble enough for savouring
Hector's high smoke.
    Next to her detestation of the Trojans,
My wife likes baiting me:
    'So you have helped the Dribbler *again*,'
That is how Hera styles my favourite king,
Priam of fountained Troy,
A stallion man—once taken for myself—
Who serviced 50 strapping wives from 50 towns,
Without complaint—to unify my Ilium,
Though all she says is:
    'From where I sit your city on the hill
Stinks like a brickfield wind.'
    I tell you, Thetis, Hera is Greek mad.
Unable to forget that Paris judged her less—
Nudely speaking—than Lady Aphrodite;
Hates my best boy, poor, pretty, Trojan Ganymede;
And hates his city, too.
    Better leave now. Before she sees us talking.
Go. I nod. I answer Yes,"
Adding (but only to himself): "In my own way—
And in my own good time."

Then hitched his robe and strolled towards his court.

•

Hard as it is to change the interval
At which the constellations rise
And rise, against their background dark,
Harder by far, when Zeus inclines his head

And in the overlight his hair
Flows up the towering sky,
To vary his clairvoyance. "Yes,"
He has said. Yes, it will be, and

    Now,
In a hoop of tidal light,
The lesser gods observing his approach,
Approach, then wait, then bow, and then
Lit by their deferential eyes
Conduct the King of Heaven through his park,
Enthroning him, and at his glance, themselves;
Except for her, his sister-wife, Queen Hera, who
Puts her face close to his, and says:

    "Warm lord,
Have you ever seen a camel led by a crab?
If not, look here"
(Widening her eyes' malicious lazuli)
"And view yourself.
    Not that I am surprised. Oh dear me, no.
The moment that my back is turned—plot-plot, plan-plan,
Which I, of course, will be the last to hear of.
    That salty Thetis has been at your knees.
Not a god's god, I know. But curved.
    What did you nod to as she left?
Just because all creation knows
Fig Paris with the curly-girly hair
Refused Athena and my humble self
Does not mean you can leave us ignorant."

    "First Heart," God said, "do not forget
I am at least a thousand times
Raised to that power a thousand times
Stronger than you, and your companion gods.

What I have said will be, will be,
Whether you know of it, or whether not.
   So shut your mouth
Or I will kick the breath out of your bones."

   And Hera did as she was told.

   It was so quiet in Heaven you could hear
The north wind pluck a chicken in Australia.

   And as she reached her throne, she bit her tongue;
And when her son, the crippled Lord of Fire,
Came gimping up to her and said:
   "Mother?"
She turned away,
   "Mother?"
Then turned the other way, and would have said:
   "Not now.
I have enough to bear without the sight of you,"
Except her mouth was full of blood.
   "Mother,
You are quite right to be ashamed of me,
For you are large, and beautiful, while I
Am small and handicapped."
   And as she could not speak unless she gulped,
Just as she gulped, Hephaestus put
A jug that he had struck from frosted iron,
Then chased, in gold, with peonies and trout,
Into her hand, and said:
   "Forget God's words.
Spring kisses from your eyes.
Immortals should not quarrel over men."
Then, turning on his silver crutch
Towards his cousin gods, Hephaestus
Made his nose red, put on lord Nestor's voice,

And asked:
    "How can a mortal make God smile?"

(Two . . . three . . .)

"Tell him his plans . . ."

    And as their laughter filled the sky
Hephaestus stood remembering how, one day
Angered at some mistake of his,
God tossed him out of Heaven into the void,
And how—in words so fair they shall forever be
Quoted in Paradise: "from morn
To noon he fell, from noon to dewy eve,
A summer's day, and with the setting sun
Dropped from the zenith like a falling star
On Lemnos" in an arc that left
Him pincer-handed with crab-angled legs.

    And Hera recognized
The little jug's perfection with a smile,
As on God's arm, the lesser gods their train,
Starlit they moved across the lawns of Paradise,
Till them to him, till him to them, they bowed
Goodnight; and soon, beside his juno queen,
Zeus lay asleep beneath the glamorous night.

    And so to Troy.

2

"Who's there?"
"Manto, sir."
"Manto?"
"Yes, sir. Your youngest son."

"Shine the light on your face.

"Come here.

"Now wipe my mouth.
No-no-no-no-no-no. Take it from there.
I like a clean one every time."

Skirts graze.

"Ah, Soos . . ."

The curtain rings.

"Soos, this is my youngest son.
Soos is my herald, son. He must be . . ."
    "80, sire."
"And you are?"
    "11, sir.
Queen Neday's child."
    "Of course.
Your mother was my eighth, full, wife,
Resigned to . . . Soos?"
    "Lord Rebek, sire.
Queen Hecuba's first nephew."

Others come.

·

"Now, Manto—tell me truthfully:
Have you killed your first Greek?"
    "I think so, sir. Today.
When the car stopped I shot one in the back."
    "Who had the reins?"
    "The Prince Aeneas, sir."

A pause. A look at Soos. And then
King Priam stands:
    Some six foot six; indigo-skinned; his brush-thick hair
Vertical to his brow; blue-white:
Correctly known as the Great King of Troy;
Who says:

"Aeneas is no more a prince than you a king.
He is Anchises' son, not mine.
Anchises cannot sire a prince.
Lords—yes; but princes—no.
    You, Manto, might—note I say *might*, Soos—"
    "Sire—"
    "Be king of Phrygia one day, and tax
My hilltop cousin, lord Anchises, of some beef.
But that is all.
    So do not trust the gods too much, young man.
Gods fail their worshippers—but not themselves."

"Your chair is here, sire."

Priam turns.

They go.

Like monumental wings
The doors that overlook the acropolis' main court
Open onto the evening air
And Priam's portico.

And when his chair appears
(With four sons walking by each arm)
Neomab, Soos' next, declares:

"All rise for Priam, Laomedon's son,
Great King of Troy, and Lord of Ilium."
Old Priam seats his Council of 100 with his hand,
Gathers his strength, and cries:

"Where is my son? My only son?
I do not see my son! He has no twin!
Take all my sons, Achilles, but not him,"
But only to himself.

Aloud, he says:

"I reign with understanding for you all.
Antenor, as the eldest, will speak first.
    Our question is:
How can we win this war?"

"And I reply," Antenor, standing, says,
"How can we lose it?
    God's Troy has been besieged a dozen times
But never taken.
    Your line goes back 900 years.
The Greeks have been here nine. Surely their chance

49

To take your city worsens in the tenth?"
    (Anchises' face is stone.
His kinsman, Panda, spits.)
    "If we have difficulties, so do they;
If we are tired, so are they;
And we are tired at home. Behind our Wall.
    These are their facts:
Full tents, thin blankets, gritty bread,
With agitators poulticing their weariness.
    And one thing more: they have a case.
Their law of hospitality is absolute.
You are a guest, you are a king. The house is yours.
    Paris—may God destroy him—was Menelaos' guest
And Helen was / is Menelaos' wife.
He wants her back. Greece wants her treasure back.
Neither unreasonable demands.
Women are property for them.
And stolen property can be returned."

    Panda would interrupt, but Meropt—
Aphrodité's priest—restrains him.

    "My king,
The winners of a war usually get
Something out of it.
    What will we get?
Their camp. Their ditch. And who wants those?
Only Lord Koprophag, the god of shit.
    Dear my dear lord, some here would garrison the clouds
In case we are invaded from the moon."

    Impatient now:

    "Stand Helen on a transport piled with gold—
Supplied by Paris—covered with silk,

Frogged with pearl—likewise supplied.
And as they rumble through the Skean Gate
Let trumpets from its terracing
Bray charivari to her long white back's
Disgusting loveliness."

Applause.

And under it:
"Where can that Hector be?" the old king asks.
  "On his way here, sire. From the Temple."
As Antenor ends:

"Achilles is no different from the rest.
Let him face stone. Sixty by thirty feet of it.
Height before width. Our dam. The Wall. The death of Greece.
Keep its gates down and send our allies home.
Since men have lived, they lived in Troy.
Why fight for what is won?"

Now more—too much —applause,
Into the last of which:

"This is the why," Anchises, lord of Ida, said
As Panda and Didanam
(Panda's bow-slave) helped, then held him up:

For 60 years ago
As he was swimming in Gargara's lake
My Lady Aphrodité glimpsed his buttock's cusp
And had him in a drift of asphodel.
  That done,
She pushed his hair back off his brow
And took his hand and spoke to him by name:

"Anchises, I am fertile.
Our son, who you will call *Aeneas*, shall be king.
But cite our bond to anyone but him,
You will be paralysed from the waist downwards.

Gods always ask too much.
Just as Anchises said, "This is the why,"
One day he grinned at those who claimed
A new-bought templemaid to be
    "As good as Aphrodite," and said:
    "She's not. I know, because I've had them both."
And as they laughed shrivelled from hip to foot.

Withered or not:

"This is the why," Anchises said.
"Troy is not Ilium. And without Ilium
Troy will not last.
    You say: 'Give Helen back, they will go home.'
O sorry orator, they have no home.
They are a swarm of lawless malcontents
Hatched from the slag we cast five centuries ago,
Tied to the whim of their disgusting gods,
Knowing no quietude until they take
All quiet from the world; ambitious, driven, thieves;
Our speech, like footless crockery in their mouths;
Their way of life, perpetual war;
Inspired by violence, compelled by hate;
To them, peace is a crime, and offers of diplomacy
Like giving strawberries to a dog.
    Indeed, what sort of king excepting theirs
Would slit his daughter's throat to *start* a war?"

King Priam yawns.

"They must be beaten. Preferably, destroyed.
Return their she, her boxes, they will think:
'Ilium is weak'—and stay. Retain them, they will think:
'Ilium is fat'—and stay. As either way
They want your city whole; your wives,
Your stuff and stock, floodlit by fire, while they
Pant in their stinking bronze and lick their lips.
    Ask who you like from Troy Beyond.
The Dardanelles, Negara Point,
Arisbe, Hellespont, then south,
Hac, Paran, Tollomon, and then Kilikiax,
Inland as far as Thebé-under-Ida,
Seaward to Chios and to Samothrace,
All say: 'For us, the time to die is ripe,' and have
Nothing to spare except their injuries.
'And where is Troy?' they ask. 'We paid her well,
Great Priam had our princess for a queen,
Turns his back now, sends our allies marching home,
As if Pe'leus' son was just a name.'

    "Ask Hector's wife. Andromache has lost
Her sire, King Etion, four brothers, and their town,
Shady Kilikiax, at Achilles' hands.
She will not underestimate the lad's ferocity.
    He is what they call Best. That is to say:
Proud to increase the sum of human suffering;
To make a wife, a widow; widows, slaves;
Hear, before laughter, lamentation;
Burn before build.
    Our only question is:
How best to kill him? Panda has planned for that.
    The saying goes:
Not the dog in the fight but the fight in the dog.
And you, Antenor, have no fight.
You speak from cowardice. You plan from fear."

Then Panda's "True!" was mixed with someone's "Shame..."
"Shame..." merged with "Answer him..." and "Fool..." with "Stand..."
Their voices rising through the still, sweet air

As in the spring of 1961
Elly and Hugo Claus and I
Smoked as we watched
The people of the town of Skopje
Stroll back and forth across their fountained square,
Safe in their murmur on our balcony,
One dusk, not long before an earthquake tipped
Themselves and their society aside.

Now,
Almost by touch, the Council's tumult died, as
Gowned, down the flight of steps that joins
Temple to court, surrounded by Troy's dukes,
His sacrifice complete, Prince Hector comes.

Whether it is his graceful confidence,
His large and easy legs and open look,
That lets him fortify your heart,
That makes you wish him back when he has gone,
Trusting oneself to him seems right, who has belief,
And your belief respected, where he stands.

"My son!"

No sound aside from Priam's cry, as Hector led

Chylaborak,
Andromache's one brother left, King Etion's heir,
Across the courtyard; plus
Aeneas,
Brave, level-headed, purposeful,

Treated by Ida's herdsmen as a god;
  Troy's Lycian allies,
Glaucos, beside his prince, Sarpedon;
Anaxapart, Sarpedon's armourer;
  And more
As valiant, as keen for fame, the plumes of Ilium,
That you will meet before they die,
Followed their Hector up, onto the portico
Before the monumental wings, and stood
Around the king, who pulls his son's face down,
And kisses it, even as he whispers:
  "Where have you *been*?"

And Hector lets the smile this brings
Fade from his lips, before he says:

  "My friends,
Your faces bear your thoughts. Change them for these:

  "My name means 'He who holds.'
Troy; Ilium; Troy Beyond; one thing.
  The victory is God's.

  "Anchises harms the truth
By making it offensive;
Antenor hides the truth by making out
Greece has already lost.

  "God break the charm of facts!
Excepting these:
That we are sick and tired of the Wall.
Of waking up afraid. Of thinking: Greece.
Your life in danger all your life. Never to rise
Alone before the birds have left their nests,
Then ride through sunlit, silent woods,

Deep snow to spring flowers in a single day,
And then, the sea . . .
  To miss these things,
When things like these are your inheritance,
Is shameful.

  "We are your heroes.
Audacious fameseekers who relish close combat.
Mad to be first among the blades,
Now wounded 50 times, stone sane.
And we will burn Greece out.
  Achilles' name, that turns you whiter than a wall,
Says this: although his mother is a god,
He is a man, and like all men, has just one life,
Can only be in one place at one time.
  It will be plain to see whose part Heaven takes;
If God guides Hector's spearcast, or if not;
If God is pleased with Hector, or if not;
If not, it is a manly thing, an honourable thing
To die while fighting for one's country.
  Be sure:
I know it is the plain that leads
Us to their ships, and them to the sea.
And when God shows the moment we should strike
I will reach out for it.
  But I—
Not you, Anchises, and not you, Antenor—
Will recognize that moment when it comes.

  "All to their towers.
Sleep tight. But do not oversleep,
Or you may miss your full Greek breakfast."

  Did our applause delay him?
Out of the corner of his eye, Chylaborak

Sees a strange herald cross to Neomab and Soos,
Then Soos make not-now signs to Neomab,
Then Neomab, apologizing with a shrug,
Go to Priam and his dukes, who ring him, and
(While our silence holds) listen, then nod.
Then face ourselves just before Soos declares:

   "Cryzez of Tollomon sends this news:
Achilles has walked out on Greece.
Tomorrow he sails home."

   "So I am right!"
   "So I am right!"
In unison, Antenor and Anchises called;
And so again, as in that fountained square,
"True," "Shame," "Right," "Answer him," and "Stand"
Became the crosstalk of their dark, that grew
Slowly and slowly less, until
All were as quiet as children drawing.

   Then Hector said:

   "Listen to me, and take my words to heart.
This changes nothing.
   I lift my hands to God,
Whose voice knows neither alien heart nor land.
He is my word, my honour, and my force.
   I shall bury Greece."

   And went.

          •

   Immediately below the parapet
Of Troy's orbital Wall, wide, house-high terraces
Descend like steps until they mill

The flagstone circus ringing its acropolis,
Whose acre top supports the palace, walk, and wall,
Rooms by the flight where Priam's 50 sons
Slept safe beside their wives before Greece came.
   The Temple faces south.
And over there
(Beyond the columns, looking down)
Notice the stairs that wind
Onto a balcony where Helen stands
And says:

   "They want to send me back."
And (taking a pastry snail from a plate
Inlaid with tortoise-shell) Paris, who caused the war, replies:

   "Heaven sent you here. Let Heaven send you back."

   While in his sleep King Priam shouts:
"You are too faithful to your gods!"

                    •

   Cut to the flat-topped rock's west side, and see
Andromache touch Hector's shoulder:

   "Love,
I am a good and patient wife.
I speak the truth. My father was a king.
Yet when he slaughtered him,
Achilles did not rubbish Etion's corpse,
But laced him in his plate and lifted him,
As tenderly I do our son, onto his pyre,
And let our 12-year-olds plant cypresses
Around his cairn, before he burnt
Leafy Kilikiax, and led them to his ships.
   Distrust cold words.

Friendship is yours, and openheartedness.
I hear your step—I smile behind my veil.
To measure you, to make your clothes,
Your armour, or to forge your blades,
Is privilege in Troy.
You fear disgrace above defeat. Shame before death.
And I have heard your bravery praised
As many times as I have dried my hands.
Be sure of it!—as you are sure of me.
As both of us are sure
Courage can kill as well as cowardice,
Glorious warrior."

  Then as they walk along the pergola
Towards the tower of the Skean Gate
Shadowed by Rimph and Rimuna, her maids,
Her wedding present from Chylaborak,
Both honoured to sleep Hector, if he chose:

  "Half Troy is under 20, love.
Half of the rest are wounded, widowed, old.
Hush . . ." raising her finger to his lips,
"Why else does Prince Aeneas take a boy
As young as Manto in his car?"

  "Aeneas is my business."

  Silence.

  Then:

  "My lord, you never yet
Treated me like a woman.
  Do not start now.
Your family quarrels are your own," and walked
Before her skirts that trailed along the floor

Before him through the horseshoe arch
Into the tower's belvedere; retied
The threads of her veil at the back of her head,
Smiled Rimuna and Rimph away, then said:
    "Dearest, nearest, soul I know,
You hesitate to fight below your strength.
Short work, therefore, to needle Hector with the thought
It was the weakness of the Greeks and not his strength
That kept them out, that kept them down, that sent them home.
But those who say so preach: not prove.
    Why, sir, even if you sent
Sarpedon, Glaucos, and Anaxapart
Back home to Lycia, Aeneas to his hills,
Prior to shouldering Agamemnon's race
Into the Dardanelles, alone,
Those preachers would not change their tune.
    Day after day I wash Greek blood off you;
It teaches me that Greece is not so far,
And not so strange, to be exempt exhaustion.
    Send Helen back.
Let her establish a world-record price.
Desire will always be her side-effect.
And Achilleus is out.
    O love, there is a chance for peace.
Take it. We all die soon enough."

    Hieee . . . Daughter of Etion,
From diadem past philtrum on to peeping shoes
You show another school of beauty.
    And while he looked
Over the Trojan plain towards the Fleet,
And thought of what Apollo, in the Temple, put
Into his heart, your Hector said:
    "I know another way,"
As moonlight floods the open sky.

3

Now all creation slept
Except its Lord, the Shepherd of the Clouds,
Who lay beside his juno queen
With Thetis on his mind.

So to a passing Dream he said:

"Go to the Fleet.
Enter its king.
Tell him this lie:
    'Strike now, and you will win.
Zeus' lake-eyed queen has charmed the gods
And thrown a great nought over Troy.'"

Disguised as Nestor's voice, the Dream
Sank into Agamemnon's upside ear, and said:

"Lord of the Shore, the Islands, and the Sea,
You know my voice. You know I speak the truth.
    You are God's king. He pities you. And is,
As always, on your side. These are his words:
    Strike now. Hero and host. As one. And you will win.
My lake-eyed queen has charmed the gods
And drawn a great nought over Troy."

And as its host awakened, the Dream died.

•

Heralds to Agamemnon's tent.
Bright apricot rifts the far black.

They bow.

"Fetch my great lords.
Then have your less assemble Greece."

And as Talthibios did,
Dawn stepped barefooted from her lover's bed
And shared her beauty with the gods,
Who are as then; and with ourselves, as now.

·

Outside.

Pylos, and Salamis, and Calydon,
Crete, Sparta, Thessaly, Tyrins, Ithaca.

Formidable.

Even a god would pause.

But not himself:

"I have important news.
An hour ago,
Dressed in your voice, dear lord of Sandy Pylos,
God came to me and said:
    'Make total war today, hero and host, as one,
Troy will be yours by dusk.'"

The dawn wind pats their hair.

Odysseus gazes at his big left toe.
His toe. Until Idomeneo said:

"Then you awoke, my lord."
"I did.
And sent for you at once."

A pause.

Then Nestor said:
"You say it had my voice?"
"It did."
"My normal voice?"
"Your normal voice."
"The voice that you hear now?"
"As now."

Nobody speaks.

"Well?"

Nobody.

Along the beach-head's eastern reach
Stentor is calling Ajax' men to the Assembly.

Then Diomed:

"My lord, excuse my age.
Young as I am I wish to ask you if,
By 'as one,' by 'total war,' you mean us lords to fight
Beside the less?"

"I do."

"My lord, I am the child of kings."

"And we are not?"

"My lord, my uncle, Meleager, slew
The mammoth hog that devastated Calydon.
My father died while fighting for your own
Against the eyeless tyrant, Oedipus of Thebes,
And his incestine heirs. In Argolis
My family lands defend the frontiers of your own.
Perhaps the Woman Prince will offer me
A glorious death beneath the walls of Troy,
Or if that is presumptuous, then at least
Wounds, without which no hero is complete,
A trumpet played into a drain.
    Of course you are delighted by the thought
Of taking Troy without Achilles,
And that our mass must fill the gap
That righteous lord has left.
    But, sir,
Why should I fight alongside my inferiors?
The mass is cowardly; a show of dirty hands,
Slop for Thersites' scrag, that have as gods
Some rotten nonsense from the East.
    Bred from the instruments of those
Our ancestors evicted or destroyed—
Bronze is for them to polish, not to wear.
Better be born a woman; leaky; liking to lose,
Or a decent horse, than one of them.
Bitter but better, fetch Pe'leus' son,
Tiptoe around him, pick one's moment, plead,
Than share our triumph with our trash."

Everyone looks in a different direction.

Then Nestor said:

"Paramount Agamemnon,
Had anyone except yourself so dreamt
I would have begged him not to mention it.
But as things are, we will inspire
Both lords and less to fight for you.
　　As for yourself, young sir,
Remember that I fought beside your father.
He would say this:
　　What Heaven has ordered, Heaven can change.
If God says total war, total it is."

·

See sheep in Spain: the royal flock,
Taking five days to pass you as they wind
White from their winter pasture, up,
Onto the Whitsun prairie of Castile,
Wrinkle its brow, and weed, with even pace,
That sunny height; so that their collies seem
To chase the passing sky.

　　Muter than these
But with as irresistible a flow
The army left its lines and walked
Over the slipways, in between the keels,
Along the camp's main track beside the ditch;
And Stentor's less settled them round the sand.

Still.

Talthibios:

"Absolute silence for the Son of Atreus,
Agamemnon of Mycenae, King of Kings."

No warmth in the sun,
As yet.

"Soldiers!" he said.
"Dressed in lord Nestor's words, our Lord and God,
Whose voice dethrones the hills,
Entered my head an hour before the dawn.
    These were his words:
    'Yours is the greatest army ever known.
Assault Troy now. Hero and host. As one.
And by this time tomorrow all its flesh
And all its fat will be your own to stow
As you prepare to sail for home; for I, your God,
As I have ever been, am on your side.'"

    After nine years,
No throat that did not ache, then would not cheer,
Hearing such things.
    Yet as hope rose, so did Thersites,
And in his catchy whine said:

    "King,
God may be on your side. But if he is on mine,
Why is Troy still standing over there?"
    Then capped our titter: "How—
Us being the greatest army ever known,
Though we outnumber Troy by three to two,
Have we not won the war?
    As for our sailing home,
Review the Fleet with me—but, O my lord,
Please do not fart. You are a powerful man,
And perished sails blow out. Then, when,

Us having scanned the shrouds, my lord,
You stroke your chin and rest your expert eye,
Resist the urge to lean against a mast,
They are so rotten you can push a walking-stick
Clean through them."

"True."
"True."

As he wades through our knees
Down to the front.

Will he step out?

He does.

He says:

"Son of Atreus, you astonish me.
You ask the Greeks to fight in a main vein for you,
Yet rob the man our victory depends on.
    What do you want?
More bronze? *More* shes? Your tents are full. And yet,"
Turning to us, "who was the last man here to hear
Lord Agamemnon of Mycenae say: 'Have this'—
Some plate—'brave fighter' or 'share this'—
A teenage she.
    One thing is sure,
That man would be surprised enough to jump
Down the eye-hole of his own knob.

    "Why laugh?
Achilles is not laughing.
The lords have let their king grab his mint she.
Nor is Achilles cross. Achilles shows restraint.

If he did not"—back to the king—"my lord,
You would be dead."

   Our shoulders rise and fall.
Something is going to happen. Soon.
   And from the middle sand Thersites shouts:

   "I have important news.
God is on Agamemnon's side.
And on the side of his great underlords.
   Comrades in arms with God, why,
Such a team can take Troy on its own,
And need not share its triumph with its trash.
   So—tea to his tablespoons—
As he needs us no more than our Achilles needs
Snot on his spearpole—we are free to go.
Go where? Go home," and here some run to him:
"Go home at once. The host. As one,"
And raise his hands: "By noon we can be rowing,
Seeing this hopeless coast fade,"
Hold his fists high, as:

   "Home . . .
   Home . . .
   Home . . ."

   We answered him,
All standing now, beneath:

   "Home . . .
   Home . . ."

   All darkened by that word,
   As sudden gusts
Darken the surface of a lake; or passing clouds

A hill; or both, a field of standing corn,
  We flowed
Back through the ships, and lifted them;
Our dust, our tide; and lifted them; our tide;
Hulls dipping left; now right; our backs, our sea;
Our masts like flickering indicators now;
Knees high; "Now lift . . ." Knocked props. "Now lift again . . ."
And our relief, our sky; our liberty;
As each enjoyed his favourite thoughts; his plans;
And to a Trojan watcher we appeared
Like a dinghy club, now moored on mud;
Now upright on bright water; and now gone.

●

So Greece near crowned its fate and came safe home,
Except the gods,
Whose presence can be felt,
For whom a thousand years are as a day,
Said: "No."

Quicker than that,
At Hera's nod Athena stood beside Odysseus
And ran her finger down his spine.
  Aoi!—see him move,
Taking his driver, Bombax, into their flight
Like flight; and saying: "Wrap that dog," hand
Bombax his crimson boat-cloak, and then leap
Onto a tilting deck and spread
His big bare feet, and cast
His landslide voice across the running beach.
  And she,
Athena of the slate-flecked silver eyes,
Divided lord Odysseus' voice

Into as many parts as there were heads.
So each lord heard:

"You are the best. You hold your ground.
You were born best. You know you are the best
Because you rule. Because you take, and keep,
Land for the mass. Where they can breed. And pray. And pay
You to defend them, you to see custom done.
You lead the less. You hold your ground."

So that mass heard
Odysseus' charming voice:
    "Be fair. The plague has gone."
His wise:
    "Even if all Thersites says is true . . ."
His firm:
    "The lords are going to stay."
His practical:
    "You know the sea?"
His hard:
    "Kakhead, get back into your place."

Hearing these things, the soldiers slowed,
Looked at each other's faces, looked away,
Looked at the water, then about, and turned,
Re-turned, and turned again,
Chopping and changing like a cliff-stopped sea
Whose front waves back into the one behind
That slaps the next, that slaps.

Bombax has got
Thersites in Odysseus' cloak
And roped it round.
    And as he humps it up the beach,

It starts; and those who watch it pass
Feel scared.

·

There is a kind of ocean wave
Whose origin remains obscure.
Such waves are solitary, and appear
Just off the cliff-line of Antarctica
Lifting the ocean's face into the wind,
Moistening the wind, that pulls, and pulls them on,
Until their height (as trees), their width
(As lands), pace that wind north for 7,000 miles.

And now we see one!—like a stranger coast
Faring towards our own, and taste its breath,
And watch it whale, then whiten, then decay:
Whose rainbow thunder makes our spirits leap.

Much like its suds the shamefaced Greeks returned
Along the many footpaths of the camp
And ringed the sand.

Some minutes pass.

And then,
With his big, attractive belly rounded out
And just a trace of dark grey hair
Ascending and descending to his cloth,

Odysseus,

Half casually,

Holding a broomstick cane,

Half casually,

Walked over to the still
Occasionally jerking item Bombax dropped
Some minutes past
Onto the middle sand.

Then:
Stoop—
Stand—
Heave—
Lift—
Odysseus slewed Thersites out:
Who knelt; who tried to slip his gag; then did.

"Speak out," Odysseus said.
"Think of your crowd.
As they brought you to life,
Because of you they see themselves
As worthy of respect. To have a voice.

"No?

"Not a word.

"You must have something to complain about."

No sound.

"Then, there, old soldier, I can be of help."

And raised the cane and gave Thersites' neck,
Nape, sides, back, butt, stroke after slow, accurate stroke,
And pain, lewd pain, a weeping pain, your smash-hit,
High-reliability, fast-forward, pain.

Then passed the rod to Bombax,
Took back his cloak, helped poor Thersites up, and said
Softly to him, but also to our selves:

"Back to your place, Greek,
Let me hear that voice of yours again
And I will flog you, naked, from lord Ajax' ships
At one end of our beach, to lord Achilles' at the other."

As for Thersites
Our shoulders parted, and he sat
Touching his welts with one
And with the knuckles of his other hand
Wiping his tears away.

And as it is with soldiers,
Sad as we were a laugh or two went up,
As one nod murmured to the next:

"He went too far."
"I told you so."
"You must admit Odysseus talks sense."
"And what a fighter!"
"Bombax, too."
"A lovely man."
"Shush . . . shush . . ."

For having joined the greater lords
And, at Agamemnon's nod, taken the mace:

"Odysseus is about to speak."

Some say the daylight sharpens where he stands
Because Athena guards him:

"So she does."

And so we see her now,
Like an unnamed, intelligent assistant
Standing a touch behind him, on the left.

Talthibios says:

"That those far off may hear as well
As those close to, full silence for
Prudent Odysseus, the lord of Ithaca."

Who keeps his eyes well down
And turns his words towards King Agamemnon.

Gulls.

"True king," Odysseus said,
"No Greek believes more firmly than myself
That all occasions are at God's command.
    As God gave you, our king of kings, to us,
So you are given the best of all we take,
And you, through Heaven, ensure due custom done."

"Well said . . ."

    "Remember then"—turning his voice on us—
"You who believe the last thing that you heard;
Who tell yourselves you think, when you react;
Captains in camp, but cowards on the plain;
Keen to be off, but frightened of the sea—
You are not king. You never shall be king.
You see a hundred Agamemnons. God sees one,
And only one. Who bears the mace. Who speaks his word.
Who cares for us.

So keep your democratic nonsense to yourselves,
And when your betters speak to you—obey."

Idomeneo twists a fig
Off Merionez' bunch.

"At the same time, plain common sense says:
Agamemnon knows how hard it is
For lord and less alike to be away from home,
Stuck on some island, say, no wife, no she,
Even for a month, let alone years.
   But as he knows this, so he knows
The world has no time for a king whose fighters leave him.
   Or would you have Thersites as our king?"

Swifts flit from spear to spear.

"Of course we are impatient.
That is Greek.

   Yet, as it is wrong
To be found drunk at sacrifice; and wrong
Not to hold your father in your arms;
Consider how much worse would be to row
With bowed heads home
Over the open graveyard of the sea
And then slouch emptyhanded through the door."

   "True . . ."
   "True . . ."

The gulls.

"Those with the Fleet at Aulis will recall
King Agamemnon sacrificed his child,

Iphigeneia, plus 50 bulls,
For us to have flat seas and following winds;
And when their throats hung wide
And we were kneeling by the smoky spring,
Beneath its cedar tree, before its stone,
A slug-white thigh-thick python slid
Out of the ferns that bibbed the stone,
Then glided through the lake of votive blood
And up into the tree and searched its leaves.
    Eight fledgling sparrows chirruped in those leaves;
And, as we watched, the python sucked them in,
Then snatched their mother off the air,
Tainting our sacrifice. Or so we thought.
    However, as the great snake fawned
And periscoped above the cedar's crown,
God stared into its eyes. And it was stone.
White stone. Figured with gold. Tall. Smooth white stone.
A thing of beauty from a loathsome thing."

    "Indeed . . ."
    "Indeed . . ."

    "Then he who sees is, was, and will,
Calchas, now standing over there, beside our king,
Said, as he will say once more . . ."

    Sighting his finger on that seer,
Who swallows, stands, then recapitulates:

    "The time has come for Greece to praise its God.
What we have seen means this:
    Eight young—eight years before the Wall.
But when their mother's summer ninth has come,
Victory over Hector will be ours."

78

"This is that summer," lord Odysseus called
(Leaving the anxious Calchas on his feet).
    "To waste our king's dream is to scorn our dead.
So we strike now. Hero and host. As one.
Take Troy by total war. And sail safe home."

    These were Odysseus' words.
And as he sat, Greece rose and roared:

    "Troy . . . Troy . . . Troy . . . Troy . . ."

    Echoing in the hulls, along the dunes,
And rising through that likeness, this:

    "Best do as lord Odysseus says."
    "The king is king."
    "True . . . True . . ."
    "But we were not to blame."
    "Mistaken."
    "Not to blame."
    "Quite brave."
    "Good on our feet."
    "Certainly not to blame."
    "Everyone else did . . ." ". . . did."
    "And nothing to be done about it now . . ."

    While Agamemnon stood,
And when they settled, said:

    "I thank the Lord that Greece has found its senses,
And hope it manages to keep them."
    The sea regards the sun.
    "Similar silliness
Made me begin the quarrel with Achilles
About some foreign she.

79

Well, well. God's ways are strange."
The sun, the sea.
And now the former gives a little warmth.
   "So no regrets.
This is the morning of the day
Whose dusk will see Troy won.
   The lords will join me for the battle sacrifice.
The less will eat and arm.
   Never forget that we are born to kill.
We keep the bloodshed to the maximum.
And soon, swimming in Ilium's happiness,
Each one of you will have a Trojan she
To rape and rule, to sell or to exchange,
And Greece will be revenged for Helen's wrong."

   And why, I cannot say, but as he sat
Our answering cheer was like the wave foreseen
When, crest held high, it folds
And down cloud thunders up the shaken coast.

                            •

   A hundred deep,
The lords surround their lords:
   Merionez, Idomeneo's next,
His eyes the colour of smoked glass;
   Odysseus, unthanked—but unsurprised;
   Ajax (of course), and standing by him
Little Ajax—like a side of beef—
His brother by a purchased she;
   By him their cousin, Teucer;
   Diomed, just 21;
   Thoal of Calydon, his hair like coconut,
Who always knows exactly what to do;
   And Menelaos, silent, doubtful, shy,

Watching his brother and lord Nestor lead
A huge red hog with gilded tusks into the ring.

   And all their world is bronze;
White bronze, lime-scoured bronze, glass bronze,
    As if,
Far out along some undiscovered beach
A timeless child, now swimming homewards out to sea,
Has left its quoit.

   The heroes kneel. Then lift their palms.
By Agamemnon's feet Talthibios sprinkles barley;
Snips a tuft from the hog's nape;
Waits for the breeze to nudge it off his hand
Into the fire surrounded by the heroes and their king

   Who prays:

   "Force Lord of Heaven,
O Dark, Immortal Breath,
Hold back the night until I break
Into Hector's body with my spear,
Fill Troy with fire,
And give its sobbings to the wind."

   "Pae'an . . ."
"Vouchsafe us Troy."

   Curls of high smoke
As if the air was water.
   The heroes kneel. Then lift their palms.
King Agamemnon draws his knife. Its point goes in.

   Ah me . . .
God took your hog but spiked your prayer.

Futureless spoons, his name is everywhere,
His name is everywhere. And when the barbecue
Of fat-wrapped thigh-cuts topped with lights,
And in its silver sea-dark wine, had crossed your lips,
Lord Nestor stood, and with concern for all, began:

"Today will be our longest day" but he was wrong.
    "The engineers will top
The rampart with a palisade
One pitchlength shipward from the ditch,
Which, while Thetis' son is not our front,
Will be our back,
    God stop that any Greek,
Wherever from, whatever place he holds, should die
Without hard fighting and renown.
    So no more talk.
    The king will arm. The lords will join the host,
Answering our clear-voiced heralds as they call—
From mountain fastness, riverside, or lake,
Farm, forest, lido, hinterland, or shore,
Pasture, or precinct, well, or distant wall,
By father's name, or family name, or lord's,
The long-haired Greeks to battle, with this cry:

*Lead on, brave king, as you have led before,
And we shall follow."*

    Immediately
Wide-ruling Agamemnon's voices called
Greece to its feet, and set it on the move;
    And as they moved,
To stunt-hoop tambourines and trumpet drums,
The Woman Prince, ash-eyed Athena, flew
Her father's awning, called the Aegis, blue,
Broad as an upright sky, a second sky

82

Over their shoulders rippling estuary,
    And turned the pad
Of tassel-ankled feet, the scrape of chalk
On slate, of chariot hubs, back on itself
And amplified that self; contained its light;
Doubled its light; then in that blinding trapped
Man behind man, banner behind raised banner,
My sand-scoured bronze, my pearl and tortoise gold,
And dear my God, the noise!
As if the hides from which 10,000 shields were made
Came back to life and bellowed all at once.
    See how the hairy crests fondle each other onwards as
From hill and valley, well and distant wall,
All those who answered Agamemnon's call
Moved out, moved on, and fell in love with war again.

    "KING!" "KING!"

    As shining in his wealth, toting the solar mace,
Thighs braced against his chariot's wishbone seatstays,
The Shepherd of the Host,
Lord of the Shore, the Islands, and their Sea,
God's Agamemnon in his bullion hat
Drove down their cheering front.

    "KING!" "KING!"

20,000 spears at ninety, some
scaffolding poles, full-weight, to thrust,
        moving towards Troy; some light,
surveyor rods, to throw;
10,000 helmets—mouth-hole, eye-hole, open-faced,
chin-strapped or strapless;
        "Move . . . Move . . ."
5,000 crests—T, fore-and-aft, forward curving

(though either will do), some half-moon war-horns;
        "Move . . ."
shields: posy, standard, 8-oval-8 or "tower,"
two-to-six plyhide, some decked with bronze;
bows: single curve, lip-curved, lip-curves with reflex tip
(tested, found arrow-compatible);
        "Keep up, there . . ."
blades: short, long, leaf, stainless,
haft-rivets set square :: triangular ∴ with rat-tailed tangs
(these from Corfiot workshops, those imported);
        "Chariots!"
good (hay-fed) car-mares, each with her rug
(these double as body bags);
ships: long, black, swift, how many, how full;
400 tons of frozen chicken—their heads a world away;
a green undercoat;
and reaching the top of the swell in the plain:
        "*Now* see the Wall."
barbs, barbs plus spur, spades, beaded quivers,
body-paint, paste flecked with mica, arm-rings,
chapati-wrapped olives, hemmed sheepskins
(in case it gets cold without warning)

        "KING!" "KING!"

and birth bronze, dust bronze, surgical bronze,
mirror bronze, cup bronze, dove
(seven parts copper to one part tin)
        down the hill towards Troy.

Guide to Pronunciation

Achean	Ak·**ee**·an
Achilles	A·**kil**·eez
Achilleus	Ak·ee·**lee**·us
Aeneas	An·**ee**·us
Agamemnon	Ag·ah·**mem**·non
Anchises	An·**ky**·sez
Andromache	An·**drom**·a·ki
Antenor	An·**tee**·nor
Antilochos	An·**til**·o·kos
Aphrodite	Aph·ro·**dite**
and	
Aphrodité	Aph·ro·**dye**·ti
Athena	Ah·**thi**·na
Atreus	**Ay**·tre·us
Aulis	**Aw**·lis
Bombax	**Bom**·bax
Briseis	Bri·**see**·is
Calchas	**Cal**·kas
Chios	**Kee**·os
Chylaborak	Chy·**lab**·or·ak
Clytemnestra	Cly·tem·**nes**·tra
Cryzez	**Cry**·zez
Cryzia	**Cry**·zee·ah
Didanam	Di·**da**·nam
Diomed	**Di**·oh·med
E'thyl	**Ee**·thil
Etion	Et·ee·on
Glaucos	**Glau**·cos
Hephaestus	He·**phys**·tus
Hera	**He**·rah
Idomeneo	**Ee**·dom·in·**ee**·oh
Ilium	**Ill**·ee·um

Kie	**Ky**·ee
Kilikiax	Kil·**ik**·i·ax
Koprophag	**Kop**·ro·fag
Laomedon	Lay·oh·**me**·don
Meleager	Mel·ee·**ay**·gher
Menelaos	Men·na·**lay**·us
Menotion	Men·**o**·ti·on
Merionez	Mer·**eye**·on·ez
Meropt	**Me**·ropt
Mycenae	My·**sea**·nay
Mykonos	**Mik**·oh·nos
Neday	**Nee**·day
Negara	Nee·**gar**·rah
Neomab	**Nee**·oh·mab
Odysseus	O·**diss**·ee·us
pae'an	pye·**an**
Panachean	Pan·ak·ee·an
Paran	**Par**·an
Patroclus	Pa·**troc**·lus
Pe'leus	Pe·**lee**·us
Priam	**Pry**·am
Rebek	**Re**·bek
Rimph	Rimph
Rimuna	**Rim**·u·na
Sarpedon	Sar·**pee**·don
Skean	**Ski**·an
Skopje	Sco·pee·ay
Sy'mois	**Sigh**·mois
Talthibios	Tal·**thigh**·bios
Teucer	**Tew**·sir
Thersites	Ther·**sigh**·teez
Thetis	**Theet**·is
Thoal	**Tho**·al
Tollomon	**Toll**·oh·mon
Zeus	Zoos